CANDLE BIBLE FOR LITTLE ONES

Published by Candle Books
an imprint of
Lion Hudson plc
Wilkinson House, Jordan Hill Road,
Oxford OX2 8DR, England
www.lionhudson.com/candle

ISBN 978 1 78128 141 3
e-ISBN 978 1 78128 171 0

First edition 2014

A catalogue record for this book is available from the British Library

Printed and bound in Malaysia, July 2014, LH18

Candle Bible for Little Ones

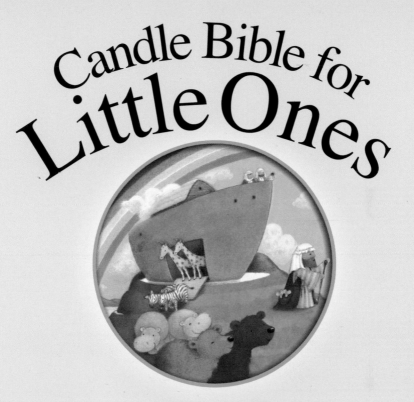

Juliet David

Illustrated by Steve Whitlow

CANDLE
BOOKS

Adam and Eve in Eden

In the beginning, God made a beautiful garden.
It was full of trees and flowers, and a river flowed through it.
Adam and Eve lived there together happily.

Until one day they disobeyed God.
Then he sent Adam and Eve out of the garden.
Their lives changed forever.

Noah and his enormous ark

God told Noah to build a huge ark
because a great flood
was coming.
Noah filled his ark
with every sort
of animal.

When the great flood came,
Noah, his family, and all the
animals were safe in the ark.
Afterwards, the ark landed on a
mountain and everyone left.
God put a rainbow in the sky.
He promised never again to
flood the world.

Joseph and his special coat

Jacob had a big family of twelve sons.
But he loved one son more than all the rest.
His name was Joseph.

Jacob gave Joseph an extraordinary coat.
How pleased Joseph was! He showed it off to everyone.
But it made his brothers very jealous.

Moses in the bulrushes

At the time Moses was born, the wicked king
of Egypt was trying to kill baby boys.
Moses' mother made a little basket, put baby
Moses inside, and floated it in the river.

The princess of Egypt came down to the river to bathe.
When she saw the baby in the basket, she loved him.
She took Moses to her palace.
There he grew up as a royal prince.

David and Goliath

David was a young shepherd boy.
Goliath was a mighty giant.
"Are you all cowards?"
Goliath shouted at David's people.
"Won't anyone fight me?"

Little David stepped forward.
He slung a stone at the giant.
Goliath fell down dead.
With God's help,
David beat the mighty giant.

Daniel and the lions

Daniel loved God. He prayed to God every day – three times.
One day the king ordered, "No more praying!"
Yet Daniel still prayed.

So soldiers threw Daniel into a pit full of hungry lions.
But God shut tight the lions' mouths.
Daniel was safe!

Jonah and the great fish

Jonah was running away from God.
He jumped in a boat and sailed away.
But God sent a storm that nearly sank the boat.
The sailors threw Jonah overboard.

Now God sent a great fish that gulped up Jonah.
After three days, the fish spat Jonah
onto the shore – safe and sound.
Jonah found out you can't run away from God.

The first Christmas

In the time of bad King Herod
there lived a girl called Mary.
One day an angel came to her.

"God is going to give you a special baby,"
said the angel.
"You must call him Jesus!"
Then the angel disappeared.

Mary was so happy!
She sang a song to thank God.

She married Joseph, the village carpenter.
They began to get things ready for the baby.

It was almost time for Mary's baby to be born.
Then the rulers of the country decided to count the people.

So Mary and Joseph had to take a long journey
to the town of Bethlehem to be counted.

At last they arrived.
Mary was feeling very tired.
Joseph knocked at the door of an inn.

"No room!" said the man.
So they had to sleep in a stable.

That night Mary's baby was born.
She named him Jesus.

The shepherds' story

In fields nearby,
shepherds were looking after their sheep.

Suddenly an angel appeared.
The shepherds were scared.
"Don't be afraid!" said the angel.
"Tonight a special baby has
been born in Bethlehem.
He will save his people."

Then crowds of angels filled the sky singing,
"Praise God in heaven!"

The angels disappeared
as quickly as they had come.
All was dark again.

The shepherds rushed off into Bethlehem.
They wanted to find the new baby!

Soon the shepherds found Mary
and Joseph in the stable.

Baby Jesus was lying
in the manger.

A new star

At the time Jesus was born,
wise men in a far country
were looking at the night sky.

"Look!" said one.
"I've never seen
that star before."

"It means a new king has been born," said a second.

"We must follow this star and find him,"
said the third wise man.

So the wise men set out on a long, hard journey,
following the star.

They came to King Herod's palace.
But the new king
was not there.

At last the star stopped over Bethlehem.

As soon as they saw little Jesus, the wise men knelt down.
They knew he was the new king.
They gave him rich presents: gold, frankincense, and myrrh.

Jesus calls Peter and Andrew

When Jesus grew up, he wanted a team to help him.
One day he saw two brothers fishing.
"Peter!" he called, "Andrew! Follow me!"

They both looked up.
"I will teach you to catch people instead of fish," said Jesus.
Andrew and Peter soon joined Jesus' special team.

A lost sheep

Jesus told this story.
Once a shepherd had
100 sheep – but lost one.
He went out to search
for his lost sheep.

At last the shepherd found the missing sheep.
He carried it home.
The shepherd was so happy that he had a party!
Jesus said, "God is just as happy when someone returns to him."

The stranger who helped

This is another story told by Jesus.
A man was on a lonely road
when robbers beat him up.
He was badly hurt.

A priest walked past.
A man from the Temple walked past.
Then a stranger stopped and helped.
Jesus said, "The best friend was the stranger who helped."

Jesus stops a storm

Jesus' friends were sailing across a lake.
Jesus was fast asleep in the boat.
Suddenly a fierce storm blew.
Jesus' friends were frightened.
He woke up. "Be still!" said Jesus.
At once the storm stopped.
The wind and waves obeyed Jesus.

Jesus feeds a hungry crowd

One day Jesus was telling stories to a huge crowd.
By evening, everyone was hungry.
But there was no food, except one boy's lunch:
five loaves and two little fish.

Jesus took the boy's food and gave it to the people.
There was enough for everyone!
This was one of the wonderful miracles Jesus did.

The first Easter

There was to be a great feast in Jerusalem.
Jesus took his twelve special friends.

Jesus borrowed a donkey and rode into the city.
The crowds grew very excited.

They shouted
and waved
palm-tree branches.

But some of the priests hated Jesus.
They began to plot to kill him.

On the day of the feast, Jesus ate a special supper with his disciples in an upstairs room.

Jesus broke bread
and gave it to his disciples.
But one disciple, named Judas,
was in the plot against Jesus.

He crept out.

After supper, Jesus took his friends
to a garden near the city.
"Stay here and pray," he said.

Jesus is taken

Jesus prayed too.
Then a crowd of Jesus'
enemies appeared,
led by Judas.

Soldiers marched Jesus away.
They took him to the ruler, Pilate.

"Jesus is making trouble," said a priest.
"He should be killed!"

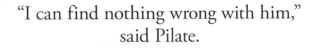

"I can find nothing wrong with him,"
said Pilate.

But the people shouted,
"Kill him, kill him!"
So Pilate sent Jesus
away to die.

A very sad day

Cruel men pushed a crown made of thorns on Jesus' head.
Then they led him out of the city.

They climbed a hill.

There soldiers put Jesus on a wooden cross.
It was between two other crosses.

Jesus said, "Father, forgive them."

At midday, the sky went dark.
Jesus cried out.
Then he died.

Jesus' family and friends
watched sadly.

A good man called Joseph
took Jesus' body.
He put it in a rock tomb
and rolled a huge stone
across the doorway.

Where is Jesus?

Early Sunday morning, some women went to the tomb.
The stone was rolled away – but they couldn't see Jesus' body.

Suddenly two shining men stood there.
"Jesus isn't here!" they said.
"He's risen from the dead."

Jesus is alive!

The women rushed off to tell Jesus' friends.
At first they didn't believe the women.

But then Jesus
appeared to them.

And after this Jesus
appeared to many
of his friends.

Once, Jesus cooked breakfast
for his friends beside a lake.

A few weeks later,
Jesus was taken up
into heaven again.

The disciples watched.

Alive forever!

At Easter, we remember that Jesus died.
And that he is alive forever.